Contents

Plant parts

Plants have
different parts.

Each part helps the plant to grow.

Roots

Most plants grow roots into soil.

root

Roots hold plants in place.
Roots take in nutrients.

Radishes are roots you can eat.
Radishes are a healthy snack!

Real Size

Real Size

A crocus is a
small plant.
Its roots are
very thin.

9

Stems

Stems hold plants up.

stem

Real size

Stems carry nutrients from the roots to the rest of the plant.

Cactuses can be large plants.

This cactus stem is covered in spines.

Real size

Dill stems are very thin.
Dill is a popular herb to eat!

Leaves

Leaves take in energy from the Sun.

Leaves make energy for the rest of the plant.

Real size

Maple trees are large plants.
Their leaves turn red and fall
off the tree in autumn.

Baby tears plants grow many small leaves. Their leaves are so small they are hard to see!

Real Size

Flowers

Flowers contain pollen.

pollen

seed

Real size

Flowers can grow seeds
for more plants.

Peony plants have large flowers.
They are beautiful colours.

Real size

Edelweiss plants have small flowers.
They grow on tall mountains.

Real size surprise!
Roses can be different sizes!

Picture glossary

 **herb** type of plant used to flavour foods

 **nutrient** something in food that living things need to grow

 **pollen** fine yellow powder made by flowers

Index

Notes for parents and teachers

Before reading
- Engage children in a discussion about plant sizes. Ask children to think of different ways we describe size, such as tall, short, wide, or thin.
- Tell children that we can use tools, such as rulers, to measure size. We can also use body parts, such as hand lengths and foot lengths, to measure size.

After reading
- Tell children that plant parts can be many different sizes. Ask children to compare the leaves on page 14 with the maple leaf on page 16. Which is larger? Encourage children to measure the leaves with a ruler.
- Using their hand as a measurement tool, have children compare the flowers on pages 20–21. How big is the peony (e.g., one hand width), and how big is the edelweiss flower (e.g., two finger widths).